A New Work Mindset

By Juan Kingsbury

ISBN Number: 978-1-716-37002-1

Author: Juan Kingsbury

Editorial Team: Jennifer Lawhead, Courtney Kingsbury, Bobby Tyning and Kate Biben.

TABLE OF CONTENTS

Foreword

Do you really want to heed advice on work mindsets from a C minus student?

Damn right you do.

Walk into most work environments and you are bound to run into a few C minus workers, if not a whole crew graded on a curve. The grade is not a reflection of them as good, well-meaning humans, but rather their performance and motivation. Imagine what they would tell you when clear headed, constructive and on your side?

So why trust me?

In 2007, I won the fulfillment jackpot when I joined international assessment provider Target Training International. Known for its multi-science and data backed assessments, I trained HR consultants and executive coaches by the 100s every year.

Prior to that, I earned an undergraduate degree in Global Business from Arizona State, and am an alum of Walt Disney World College Program. While invaluable experiences, I was unclear at the time of what was a worthy professional pursuit.

TTI's network of dominant and influential clientele was the challenge I never knew I wanted. Eventually I was tapped to work with some of the world's best executive coaches, facilitators and their high-stakes clients. Yet from high highs came inevitable lows that fueled my own excuses and finger pointing.

Culminating in 2012, with the blessing of late great founder Bill J. Bonnstetter, I created Career Blindspot to "Eliminate Workplace Excuses". I take it personally when well-meaning leaders and teams fall victim to their own excuses. As a Talent Strategist, I work with leaders to hire and develop teams that cultivate more ownership and respect at work.

I embraced my internal student/mentor that my high school self-fought yet quietly craved. I will forever deconstruct jobs, performance, and excuses. Acting as a catalyst for leaders who care about both results and people - I work with their teams to stay sharp, humble, and guide the culture on their terms.

In 2019, I started the Career Blindspot Podcast giving a platform to underrepresented leadership perspectives. As well as testing out off-center ideas with mixed metaphors and analogies that clash but may inspire other C minus mindsets.

Read this book, listen to the podcast, tell me I am wrong.

Whatever you do, do better at work.

Chapter 1
Why Can't They Do Their Damn Jobs?

"Explaining humor is a lot like dissecting a frog, you learn a lot in the process, but in the end, you kill it."
— Mark Twain

Unlike Mark's take on dissecting humor, I am going to dissect, or rather deconstruct the truth about leaders, jobs and ourselves at work.

And it will be funny! [*clenches fist]

It is up to YOU to put all of the dissected pieces back together for yourself. And then, pay it forward for the people you care about to give them *A New Work Mindset*.

Let's begin with the most commonly heard complaint around the workplace"

"Why can't people just do their damn jobs?" - All of Us

The first time I heard this line in a varied capacity was when my parents came home from work to find that people hadn't taken out the trash. Swap the word "people" with "me" (aka, their lazy son who just wanted to play Nintendo or watch pro wrestling).

When someone doesn't do their jobs, what is behind it? Laziness? Unwillingness? Arrogance? The answer is actually never black and white, even if the mind wants it to be.

Let me put it this way. We've all experienced someone who is not good at their job, right? Someone who frustrated us, let us down, lied, messed up, or was rude. The list goes on.

Why does that happen?

Humbly, I believe I know the cause and effect of the ups and downs of work mindset and attitudes. I have deconstructed them, just for you: you, leader. You, the performer. You, the human seeking more.

When you have a problem with one person around you, another team, your job role or the organization you work with, you only need one thing: a new mindset. No, a new mindset isn't just the title of this book. It's a new way to understand the truth about work.

Truly, this is really for the leaders. The "Leaders" (Capital "L"), beyond a formal title. If you are someone who's open to understanding the unique individuals who make up your workforce, I'm very excited for you. You are already a step ahead of the rest.

You care.

You have been frustrated.

Maybe confused.

Possibly burned out.

Yet, you still care.

And that makes things HARDER.

This isn't a magic pill solution (someday, c'mon science!). But the new work mindset is a framework that never fails to explain the crux of the issue. Every time someone is frustrated with a job, and especially their own, the new work mindset reveals what is going on. Every time someone wants new results, the blindspots explained will drive/prohibit the paradigm shift that so many of us seek.

I will provide clarity to frustrating situations. But most importantly, I want to assist you in harnessing your workplace frustrations and annoyances resulting from others' failures to do their job and convert that frustration into momentum...

(I was going to say "...momentum toward empowerment..." but aside from it sounding generic, it doesn't matter. What matters is, what do you want? What do you think is POSSIBLE for the people you work with, if not for yourself?)

I believe everyone secretly wants to work harder and spend more time/money - on the things they care about.

Everyone wants this, especially you.

And when we figure out what it is that you really want, amazing things happen.

However, I also believe it is NOT a requirement, nor necessary, for leaders to develop and invest in people beyond the standard needs of the job.

Why else can "poor management" exist, yet business persists?

Because it is good enough. And for many, maybe just okay.

Good may be the enemy of great but if a job pays twice a month, that is fine for many. Sure, the organization COULD be better, but does it HAVE to be better?

No.

After countless team workshops where I facilitated group discussions around personality, communication, etc., Attendees seeking "better" regularly seek me out for career advice. It goes something like this...

"Hey can I talk to you... but later. Not here."

"Sure..."

(Later)

"So, I hate my job/boss/future and you seem to understand me better than my boss. Better than myself. What should I do?"

I choose to walk a fine line to help said person, without overstepping the original client's mission and trust. After all, my client does not want to see a mass exodus of employees who discover that greener pastures not only exist but are within reach!

The majority of the time, it ends with someone understanding their situation is actually quite good. Yes, there is a lot that could be better, but the individual finds the skills they prefer to leverage are the skills their job doesn't really need/value (in that order).

That's the real cause of frustration they have been feeling.

I then explain to them that having a preference for an ability with skills that are not necessary or valued in their current position is not the organization's problem. It's THEIR problem. And more constructively, it is their OPPORTUNITY to shift how they see their current and future job opportunities.

If they were competent in their job and could persevere, I would have them consider if there could be a career path or opportunity within that company to build upon their preferred skill set. Maybe they just have the wrong seat on the bus.

After encountering many situations as described above, I started offering "career coaching" directly to help frustrated, jaded individuals invest in themselves and discover job satisfaction.

I discovered I was serving two separate yet related groups; on one end, business leaders wanting higher performers, and on the other end, individuals seeking fulfillment (aka a place where they can perform at their highest).

Whoa.

I felt, and to this day, still feel occasionally compromised yet fascinated that I'm operating on both sides of the aisle. I'm the divorce lawyer who's hanging out with both unhappy spouses. THEY KNOW IT and continue to trust me. In spite of, or maybe because of, they know I'm an equal finger pointer.

Many leaders may frown upon their people LEAVING, which is inevitable for aspiring or established high performers. However, I hesitate around "career coaching" as a descriptor since my services are not that of what a typical career coach provides: resume writing, interview prep, skill building, etc.

At the crux, I believe individuals trust and get invaluable career insights for our work together, because I understand not only their views, values and wants, but how they relate to their job. I know where they are, where they've been and the likelihood of where they'll end up. I have no crystal ball. In fact, they tell me all I need to know; I'm just really, really, REALLY good and endlessly curious at reading between the lines of what work is about and what it could be.

So many things are lost in translation, "my boss said…", "Job description reads…", or "The way I see it…"

reveal so much when you know all the variables both objectively and subjective. Fact versus opinion.

And that is the main outcome of your time investment. I aim to give you the truth about leaders, jobs, and ourselves. All of the ingredients.

We all know there are so many variables, but it is inevitable it will be overwhelming. [Shout out to anyone who's ever cooked a Thanksgiving Feast!].

I hesitated to put pen to paper about my ideas of work because I do not believe I've invented anything new. How many leadership, culture, self-help books have you read, in the last decade alone? However, with great feedback and urging from clients, mentors and friends, I accepted I have something that dents the universe for all of us who are denting, want to dent or want to support others in their denting.

DENT!!!

Apologies, back to what I hope to teach you as it relates to the OTHER end of the folks I serve: leaders. Specifically, leaders looking for more effective communication, team performance, and my favorite: hiring the right fit. Often leaders have experienced a high turnover or subpar job performance so often that they are desperate for a fresh perspective.

And that conversation usually goes like this:

"The people we hire just aren't hard working/loyal/smart/etc."

I ask, "We can learn from that, but let's focus on this job. What is the biggest problem it needs to solve?"

This question is usually met with silence; or broadly different answers.

Getting clear on the outcome is POWER-FULL.

It is where so many leaders, especially the best ones, go wrong. All the other stuff still matters – resumes, portfolios, interviews, great questions, etc. Yet, EVERY time there's underperformance or job resistance, it ALWAYS comes back to someone, if not many people, who is not being clear what needs to be done for the JOB itself.

If the skills needed for the job are unclear, that is okay. Hell, start with honesty. This is the best way to begin a search for finding a sustainable high performer. But start to look for the people who want to solve the problem you have.

The conversation always changes gears when I say, *"Let me show you the person who truly wants to regularly solve those kinds of problems every day, if not most days. Not just a person who is capable, but who wants to. They're kind of a nerd about it."*

Then it hit me: Whether I'm having the conversation with an employee or a leader, it's the same topic. Just in two different directions.

With jaded employees, I help them understand themselves first. Then we work on their understanding of the job they want versus the job they have.

With frustrated hiring managers and leaders, I help them first understand the job they want done versus the past performance. Then I give them guidance on the ideal person (or who to stay away from!).

And I'm tired of having these conversations so you all need to figure it out for yourselves.

Just kidding, I love this shit. This is the thing that I'm a nerd about. I'm going to share three major themes:

1. We often blame culture for others' unhappiness. But that's not the full story.

2. We assume everyone wants to serve a greater purpose at work. Sometimes. But not always. There are three mindsets – or three reasons we work. Understand these and you'll start to see others' motivations at work from a different lens.

3. Each of us have blindspots, five to be exact, when it comes to work. Master them and you'll go far. Ignore them and you'll likely stay stuck. If you lead others, the five blindspots will help you lead others better.

Work is complicated. It is constantly evolving and will continue to do so. Smart leaders accept that, and I want to help them.
Help you.
Let's do it.

Chapter 2
Culture is a Choice, Sorta.

I hesitated to write about culture at all, but I've seen and heard too much. Too much about what culture is, isn't, how it's great, how it's a sham, how it's a buzzword, how it's toxic…

The thing is, everyone already cares and should care more about "culture" because we all want the same thing: leaders who lead, and people who do their damn jobs.

That, my caring friends, is the culture I care about. How consistent do leaders ACTUALLY lead? And how consistent are the people they lead doing their ACTUAL damn jobs?

Culture is the ANSWER! (Hold all head nods and eyerolls, please).

Read it again: "Culture is the answer." But what was the question? One more time for the people in the back!

Leaders Actually Leading
X
People Actually Doing

= CULTURE

Culture IS the truth.

"Why aren't people doing their damn jobs?" is Spanish for, "Why aren't leaders leading?"

Even when we are not working, we see this happen regularly: at the grocery store, getting our vehicle registration and dining out at a restaurant. We see people not meeting expectations, internal or external, and the reason why ALWAYS points to who's in charge.

Of course, internally, the whole consultant world is built upon the dysfunctions of internal departments of sales, service, and operations. Sometimes isolated to each department:

- Not enough sales
- Low quality service
- Wasteful operations

And dysfunction is even more fruitful when one department is firing on all cylinders and the other cannot keep up. Or both are actually amazing but have no respect for the other.

We are humans, give yourself and others some grace.

Always and simply, dysfunction is a symptom of ineffective communication and expectation from those with authority and power.

Not so fast.

Culture isn't just blaming the leaders. Sure, the buck still stops with them. But not every great leader can save every bad attitude. Lots of stubborn capable individuals squander opportunities for a lot of reasons, briefly because they don't know what they want and they are upset others cannot figure it out for them.

A not-so-great culture is the bi-product of leaders keeping such people and attitudes at the expense of the greater mission.

It's very likely you've heard executives say, "We have a great workplace/culture because _____, _____, and _____."

Do you believe them? Do their people believe them?

Culture is the inevitable truth of leadership and the workforce's commitment to the mission.

Culture exists in every company, whether it is acknowledged or not. It's a vibe, frequency, aroma of your workplace (sometimes it stinks so bad and no one will tell you), and it spills over to vendors, customers and ultimately, the bottom line.

Culture is a reflection of an organization's REAL mission, not always the one displayed on the wall, of how their workforce relates, tolerates, or ideally lives.

What does a good culture look like?

Think of your favorite BUSINESS to experience. Think of the workers who are there to solve your problem and provide a service. They are not simply happy. They are happy to solve your problem and thorough in solving your

16

problem. They are not one track; if things go unplanned, they apologize and correct.

Great culture doesn't have to be five-star hotels.

There used to be a Taco Bell in downtown Phoenix I'd frequent. Every time I went through the drive-thru (treat yo'self!), I came out a better man. It was not always the same cashier but they always were clear, polite and just grateful to be alive; and they gave the perfect amount of hot sauce (not Fire, bleh).

And I'd always wonder, who is training these people? It was not a fluke, nor was it consistent with all Taco Bells.

Whereas premium industries are not immune to bad culture, all it takes is inconsistent values and BOOM! Two thumbs way down, three snaps in a Z-formation and a one-star review.

Example. Think of the last fancy hotel you stayed in, or a time where you took your vehicle to be serviced at the dealership. When employees have to give you lip service, do you think they really love the work they do?

Does anyone love to lie on their job?

Yes, probably, but that is just another reflection of a lacking culture for a leader who gives a damn.

And to share a full-on cliche, it starts with leadership. It is all the leader or leaders' doing/undoing.

Why?

Culture, bad to great, is heavily influenced by 3 things:

1. Consistency in values.
2. Workforce relationship to their role(s).
3. Leader's relationship to their role(s).

In no particular order:

1. Consistency in values. Consistency in values is more than just having values or posting them in the lobby. It is not even about having great values. Sticking to them, or more honorably, addressing inconsistency in values is what earns respect externally and internally.

Letting things slide, special cases and personal favors all chip away at consistency in values. I'm not claiming evil but if some know the values/rules don't apply, it is a quick way to slide into a negative environment.

If you go to any Disney theme park, you are guaranteed a magical experience. Why, because they sprinkle fairy dust on everyone? YES! This AND they train their CASTMEMBERS (WDWCP 2001 Alums waddup!) on how to provide every single GUEST with a consistent MAGICAL experience. Disney is the king of consistency.

Missteps happen but acknowledgements and correction are encouraged and even guaranteed.

An inconsistent culture: this may be viewed as a low blow, but those of you leaders who care will take it the right way – exists in many medical professional offices. When we as patients feel unheard, talked down to, or forgotten about, a DO NO HARM oath seems flimsy.

Again, missteps happen but true acknowledgement and corrective action are missing from far too many of our medical experiences.

Is that the fault of the front desk receptionist? The office manager? The nurse practitioner? The doctor?

You know what I want to know: "who's in charge and what do they ACTUALLY value?"

I'm not claiming good thoughtful values aren't worth something, but if you refuse to stick to them, your people, your workforce and your customers see it more clearly than you think. It influences in all directions.

Being clear, owning up to inconsistencies and not apologizing, but learning from, and doing better, EVERY time is how we earn (or lose) credibility and trust.

2. Workforce relationship to their role(s). A workforce relating to their roles is a no brainer for explaining how strong a culture is. People who do not like their jobs do enough to not get fired. People who love what they do, or are merely good at it, tend to deliver better results regularly.

Duh. So why so much turnover, underperformance and stress!? Easy, man!

Were you always a superstar in every role you had, every day? Yes, me too!

But now that we are done lying to each other, my truth is I was a toxic employee on several occasions. No one ever said this to my face, but I stirred up things on the job that were not mine to stir.

Blame it on age, lack of experience or maturity. I did it, and I've since learned from it. But it took some time, distance, and a lot of honesty on my reality distortions.

How does toxicity start?

Toxic behavior usually comes after a sting of being a high performer: confident, capable and getting praised regularly. Then one day, the overconfidence morphs into thinking you know best. Company time is spent going AGAINST what leadership said they wanted or prioritized.

*"You either **die** a **hero**, or you live long enough to see yourself become the villain." - Harvey Dent, The Dark Knight.*

I'm sure that quote is far older than the umpteenth batflick but it hits.

Most of us see ourselves as the hero of our own story. Our ego needs to simply survive, and many of us, while we may not use the word "victim", have played that card when fingers are pointed our way. Yet, how many of us walk into work every day and give our best Tony Montana?

"SAY HELLO TO DA BAD GUY!"

We just do not see, or acknowledge, ourselves as the problem. Yet we usually know deep down what the organization, department, specific job demands on any given day needs from us. A toxic employee just no longer cares.

What everyone does care about is solving problems, THEIR way. The closer their problem-solving approach is to what the job NEEDS, the better. It is not just business. It is personal. It's always personal.

When people LIKE solving the problems that their job presents them with EVERY DAY, you inevitably see more positive attitudes emerge. How often do you see a sad firefighter?

I'm sure it's possible, but when an unsatisfied employee knows and is ready to put out their own "fires" – the ones that a person expects and trains for every day – that's fulfillment. (More in the next chapter).

But when an employee dreads solving the problems, they are being PAID to solve, that sentiment seeps, if not soaks, the workplace relationships from top to bottom.

As you can see, it's a person's relationship to their own role that influences culture.

3. Leader's relationship to their role(s). Leadership relating to their roles is the same as workforce, but...

It's a giant but. A big ole BUT. But... it sets the tone. Leaders either protect or enable. Leaders either encourage or discourage. It starts and ends with leaders. You.

Leaders are the bookends of culture. Leaders are also the books in between, the meat, the salami in the sandwich (just go with it: a book sandwich!). A leader's relationship to their OWN role determines the strength of the bookend support.

That's why culture is a choice. Sorta.

Leaders set the tone and empower or limit their culture's potential. It's on them, you, us to keep things consistent.

Always.

Refer to your favorite local business where they have earned your trust and exceeded expectations. On the few times an error occurs, they jumped on it, corrected it, and thanked you for your patience, if not more.

For me, that is any of my family's favorite restaurants we frequent in Phoenix. (Bonus dumplings or guacamole never hurt either! Guacamole Dumplings!?)

For an inconsistent or negative culture, recall the last service or organization that disappointed you or worse, left you irate. The kind of experience that pushes you to give a scathing online review or call them out on social media.

Ask: how has leadership set the tone and empowered their front line to handle, fix, or correct your issue? They probably haven't.

If you, as a leader, do not have a good relationship with your role, here's where you can start.

First, give yourself some space/grace/truth. Leading is exciting but that also means scary, hard, and yes, when done with a clear head, incredibly fulfilling. But a deep undertaking nonetheless.

Second, if you don't have a strong relationship with your own [leadership] role, what do you REALLY expect from your workforce? You set the tone, and the bar.

I've seen and will continue to see high potential/performers embrace their roles more than their leaders, and it ultimately leads to burnout and someone destined for greener pastures.

It's not wrong or evil, nor is it mandatory. Nor does it need to be that way.

However, to be mindful of culture, is to understand it's the LEADERS who set the tone by relating to their own roles. In turn, it shapes how the WORKFORCE relates to their own individual roles (or don't... you've seen it).

Ultimately, it sets the trend of how consistent organizational values are followed today, and will be followed tomorrow.

Culture either grows or is limited by the choice leaders have with their own roles. But first, we have to acknowledge the reasons why people work. It's not linear, it's ever-changing and that's OK.

Chapter 3
The 3 Reasons We Work

Now that you know a lack of motivation cannot always be blamed on a bad culture, what other factors are at play?

I like to answer this by taking a macro and a micro perspective. This chapter is all about the macro – the 3 Reasons We Work. We'll get to the micro later.

Why do most people go to work?

Why do HAPPY/FULFILLED people go to work?

What makes up culture, the bi-product of consistent values (or not), workforce doing their actual jobs (or not), and leaders leading (or not)?

Complicated questions with complicated answers. But I attempt to simplify it in A New Work Mindset because it's important to drill down to what motivates someone to show up every day and perform.

We work to (*discovered in the book, *Go Giver*):

1. **Survive**
2. **Save**
3. **Serve**

That's it. Before we expand on the three reasons, what they mean and how they show up at work, there are a few things to consider:

1. We ALL go through them.
2. They are not necessarily linear. We may bounce between the different reasons several times in one year, depending on circumstances.
3. Some of us are stuck/over focused in one area. That's inevitable.
4. No reason is better than the others, really.
5. Fulfillment/happiness comes from embracing them all and knowing they are all at play.
6. Leaders/companies mislead.

1. SURVIVE.

"Don't die: Hunter/Gatherers need only apply." - The Original Job Description

Survival was the first reason to work and for many today, it's the only reason.

I use the square, as it is a reliable yet unexciting shape (apologies to all squares!) Do consider: how many perfectly square homes have you been in lately?

It is a reliable shape though. It gets the job done in terms of shape representation. It's basic, lacks style and is not very fancy. Just like surviving. Yes, a square seems to convey the primitive feeling of if you will stay alive, or if death awaits?

Dang Juan, getting dark.

Survival might not be our actual reality, but it certainly FEELS that way. Let's explore the feeling of being in survival mode.

Have you ever paid for groceries (your only food for the next two weeks) with the swipe of a debit card, only to be told that your card was denied? THAT is the feeling I am talking about.

The thing about surviving, even if you have been there before and struggled to put food on the table, is it is hard to relate when you are not actually in it.

When you work to survive, there is not much time for much else.

It is hard to be happy or fulfilled when you are in survival mode, you after all are focused on surviving. That stress and pressure is scary; it is not about your passion, or education or personality. All of this feels frivolous. It is simply about surviving to the next day or next paycheck. Rinse and repeat.

Many of us in the world may not be running from animals, but the realities of working to survive come to us all but in vastly different ways.

Surviving is not a bad thing. In fact, most of us will be in this position many times in life.

25

Suddenly, that job you lost that you hated didn't seem so bad because it was a steady paycheck.

Survival is a necessity, yes, and we have to figure out how to do it. There will be times we come back to it and need to focus on basic life necessities. Survival mode can also be a mindset we can get stuck in, even when a job and steady paycheck returns.

Remember, no one goes to college, enlists in the military or learns a trade just to survive. Right?

Right. They usually want more.

2. SAVE.

"Work hard, get stuff." - The Modern Goal

When you work to save, you no longer are working because you are panicked about paying the bills. You work for the "extra" – extra money, extra time and extra resources.

Things like a second car, home, vacation, health insurance, etc.

Not judging what one considers extra, but there's a big difference from working to survive (you NEED water) versus save (you WANT a beer). One has you desperate, and the other has you buzzed.

It feels good knowing you have a surplus. Extra. It is not about making ends meet. You can invest and buy things because you WANT them, not solely because you or someone you love life depends on it.

You can plan for the future, invest your money to have more money and retire one day, not having to work for money but have your money work for you. And all the other catchphrases financial planners hope you achieve.

Even the most hippie, tree-hugging 20-something wants to work to save. They may not see it that way and describe it as, "I just want enough to survive..." Ha! I hear you 20-year-old Juan, you silly, silly fool. I was not a tree-hugger, but I thought money did not matter. Until it did. Until I didn't want to just survive anymore.

Working to save is NOT bad. Nor is it good.

It is merely one of the reasons we work. Many of us are good at it. By that, I mean we are clear that we work for the extra things it brings us, control over many, but not all, things and experiences.

Far more of us wish we could be, or were better at, working to save. We want the raises, the vacation time and the fat bank account at retirement. And yet, for so many, it's out of reach.

My goal here is not judgement. It is to distinguish the difference between save (whether you are good or bad at it) and surviving.

The third reason we work is also vastly different.

3. SERVE.

"Love what you do and..." - (sorry I passed out from eye rolling and gagging at the same time).

I get the idea of passion. It is true in many ways and definitely well intentioned, but that message often misses its mark, leading to one too many wishful thinkers and finger pointers. Let us table the corny and be open to a new way of looking at what it means to work to serve. This is more than just working in a non-profit and saving left-handed orphaned puppies.

To serve is to be a great human, not solely for what you do for others but how you FEEL when you do it. Doing work that is both not about the money yet scales and profits if not saves people economically.

You are working on something to the best of your abilities for people you are connected to.

Powerful but also scary.

If you have ever had "tough love" someone, you know it.

Yes, serving is wonderful but it is a "be careful what you wished for you, you just got it" situation.

I liken it to the idea of having a baby and the reality. You LOVE them radiantly but man, babies are a lot, they cost money, they cry, they turn into teenagers and get bad attitudes, they "forget" to call you on your birthday.

Babies, man.

To work to serve is to give your all to someone or something for love, belief, and not for money or power. For so many, it's a fixed point on the horizon. "Man, if I could just work to help people by doing XX, I would be serving and feel happy."

Some get there, and some don't. But it's not a linear path. More on that in a bit.

Now, a curve ball. Working to serve is NOT better than save or survive. Why, you ask?

Imagine you have THE best job ever, and you ARE SERVING and you are getting paid top dollar. You, my friend, are helping left-handed puppies learn to read.

But then...

Economic shutdown. You just got laid off. You are probably sling shotting right back to the Survive square, and you could care less about serving because you are working to survive.

A Simple Matrix

	Survive	Save	Serve
Why	To Pay Bills	To Invest & Consume	To Create

Looks Like	Maslow's Hierarchy: Food, water. Shelter and Wi-fi	Value of Talent: Time, Money Surplus and Economics	Not Obligated, never done and always Your Best
Mindset	"I Have to…"	"I can…"	"I choose to…"
Feels Like	Stress Grind Pain	Confidence Conviction Judgmental	Love Art Vulnerable
Talent Aligned	< 2/5	3/5	5/5
%	<60%	60-79%	80%+

So, why do YOU work? Why does each unique human work? Why do those who give organizations an average of 4-6 days of their life each week, work?

Some because they have to survive.

Many because they can save.

Not enough because they choose to serve.

No judgement here. This is all opportunity, for the leaders who care, and people seeking purpose.

Get right with your reasons you work - ALL of them, and you will change your world.

But…Until you do there is a **false sense of permanence** people have with their work situations. And not just that, but they also forget or don't truly realize why things were so good when they were good, and how accessible better days are.

I've also realized the limits "successful" people have. Those of us who've done really well in the SAVE area, but know something's missing. Yet the money or perks keep us around.

First off… That is NOT a bad thing!

None of the reasons we work are bad/good. They're simply YOUR reasons. And your reasons will change based on your job, life situation and a ton of other factors.

Don't believe me?

As great as it is to serve in a job every day, there's always work that MUST be done that feels different than the work that fulfills you. We do that work because we have to, but it's not so bad because it's only a fraction of the time.

This isn't about burning the bridge and camping out on Serve. Because even if you or any employee did, they eventually NEED to pay bills and mind necessities, and if they really cared of their cause, they'd be focused on what they CAN do better to be profitable/sustainable.

And if they aren't doing the above, I question their commitment to the mission.

See any religious, non-profit, or any leader who claims good intentions but detached from economic realities.

Learn to juggle. Or water plants.

That's the secret here. These 3 reasons are in competition with one another, you have to find a rhythm, and a focus on ALL:

- No one wants to die if avoidable.
- Everyone wants more if possible.
- We all want to work hard on something.

UNPOPULAR SUGGESTION - Hire for the SAVE MINDSET.

In a perfect world yes, we'd hire for the serve. Many leaders/organizations are able to do so. But here's the kicker, it's because they HAVE plenty of folks in the SAVE mindset - people who are capable of actually doing the job. Where their talent is aligned no less than 60% but closer to 80% of the time.

Alignment of 100% is unrealistic and not only a challenge to sustain, but also individual responsibility, not a leader or organizations.

It's also why every entrepreneur/risk-taker knows sales is what makes the business world go around. But the rest of us still feel uneasy when business development is just after the SALE versus highest quality SERVICE (pun intended).

Hire for the SAVE mindset, and REWARD with support in exploring the SERVE mindset.

High performers leave roles all the time. Sure, the decision to leave is often money based, but very often it is more than that.

Example: four of the NBA's more successful and talented players of the last era -Lebron James, Kyrie Irving, Kawhi Leonard, and Kevin Durant... What they all have in common is they left WINNING teams - CHAMPIONSHIP were won. They are top talented players, the best of the best, and they won: 3 of the 4 multiple championships. And they still left. They seek something that even the teams that win the most and salaries cannot offer. You can point and judge, but my opinion is one championship team's loss, is its competition's gain. Do with that as you may.

Attrition is inevitable, but is retainment really the goal?

Retaining people who do not meet expectations, say. "No thank you!"

Those leaders who keep on a bad attitude or a toxic employee, I feel for you. To be a spectator who points and says, "Fire them and get someone who will work hard and smart for you!" is EASY! To actually do it. That can be scary, like pulling over when your jalopy road trip car may not start up again, why risk it?

Well...

Would you rather have someone for 10 years, doing C- work; or someone for 3 years crushing it with A+ work even though they eventually leave for a new opportunity?

There is no right or wrong answer here. But there is what's more realistic and what is more idealistic.

Everyone is actively moving in and out of each reason they work, and the truth is being whole and fulfilled is having a healthy relationship with each, not evading one or permanently planting down in another. Biz dev can kick butt, but eventually we have to do our reports. Deep dive analytics and supercharge the brain, but eventually you'll have to present the data and speak in public.

If someone is engaged at least 60% of the time - Good enough; ideally 80% - that is not only a GREAT fit it is SUSTAINABLE when the person is aware of the difference between their WANTS and the role's NEEDS! If someone's PERSONALITY is what the job inherently

NEEDS most of the time, they'll want to keep going and manage the rest.

Unfortunately, or fortunately, depends who you are... people (especially every young generation) are really seeking that SERVE. And good for them!

The hard part is that just isn't as sustainable as a job that fulfills SAVE.

This is not about lowering expectations; it's about not waiting for the perfect moment or boss who is going to be our ultimate opportunity. Sure, they come, but for the rest of us, being pragmatic

And then there's life again - It happens. Marriage. Divorce. Kids. Deaths. Medical bills.

Things go according to plan and then they don't; people will respond in various ways (i.e., their view on their system and how it relates to their Talent will fluctuate). Like exercise or any discipline, it's not a one and done, it's a practice. At the very least a monthly check in.

So where are you? Where is your workforce? Family? Friends? Roommate? Partner?

You want better from others; you first do better for yourself. The one who cares.

Where are you NOW?

Surviving. Saving. Serving.

Accept the reality then decide if you want more, decide what you are WILLING to CHOOSE.

The final chapter will be changing our work mindsets.

It is NOT your job to save anyone. As a leader however, it is your opportunity to show people who they WANT to be and how their role can be a part of that.

Walk the walk.

34

Remember the macro and micro perspectives I mentioned at the beginning of the chapter. We've reviewed the macro approach – the 3 Reasons We Work. Now it's time to understand the micro approach – the 5 Career Blindspots – which either move us closer to work goals or hold us black.

Let's go.

Chapter 4
The Five Career Blindspots

When someone shares their work experience, and times when things didn't go their way, several themes emerge.

They aren't weaknesses.

They are blindspots.

Willing participants always acknowledge to me, "There's something there. I'm just not sure what it is."

One or more of what I call the 5 Career Blindspots are part of their issues. EVERY TIME.

In case you are part elf and have never been jaded by work, you have still seen others go through the motions of their jobs with no hint of inspiration in their faces.

They do not want to be there. Everything is forced, like throwing a surprise party for an introvert who gets overwhelmed at a six-person dinner and you've just packed their apartment with 30 people they may not even like that much.

Going through the motions is professionalism with no heart.

It looks like the wavy air tube guy in front of a car dealership. The face looks right but the soul is escaping endlessly, if it is even there at all.

It's the uncanny valley. (Non-nerds: that's when the faux/CGI human looks creepy regardless of how detailed).

It's the NPC. (Non-video gamers: these are the non-playable characters you try to chop down to see how they respond instead of playing the actual game).

We all have seen a fake smile (dust off your yearbook to see hundreds of these) versus a genuine one. And those who are tired of forcing their smile and their professionalism, the real story emerges when you ask them about it in the right way.

It's like a monsoon in Phoenix. (For non-Phoenicians, that means it never rains but when it does get your galoshes!).

Why are SO many people SO unhappy at work? When you ask this to someone who is ready to talk, the reason for their unhappiness isn't always obvious, sometimes not even to them.

These conversations start with others:
"My boss..."
"My clients..."
"My salary...."

"My stress…"

Their complaints are merely the symptoms of deeper truths.

Deeper pain. Deeper misalignment.

Yes, good people do leave bad bosses (a common reason cited for being unhappy). If a bad boss is the reason someone gives for their job dissatisfaction, I'm skeptical. When someone is clear on what they truly want, they speak in specifics and know more than just what they don't want.

It is so easy to project and just see the flaws of someone else when you are unhappy. Even good people/performers have difficulty making the most out of bad situations.

Example. When I'm personally bogged down in lame (to me) but nonetheless important business responsibilities – taxes, operations, etc. – I tend to procrastinate and fill my time judging others (my wife/friends/family) for things they haven't done.

Not cool, Juan. And frankly, it's kind of dumb. It's inevitable I must do the things I'm avoiding anyway. I want to! Not for the sake of them, but for what they allow me to do in business, like write this book.

If I am really smart, and sometimes I am, I delegate the work.

However, I don't delegate to just anyone, but someone who actually WANTS to do the work. Juan's misery is someone else's joy.

The reasons they get joy from work I hate is why I get joy from work they or others would hate. I want the work, the problems they present interests me, solving them is fun, and the cycle goes on.

Even when I am done, I will think about it later and remember it fondly, wonder and daydream about it. I will roll that experience into the next one and it will live forever inside me.

Whereas the next time I do taxes, I just want someone who will hold my hand, tell me I am pretty, it will all be okay, and we will get tamales after.

What's the difference between the fulfilling work and the not-so-fulfilling work?

Blindspots.

These 5 blindspots/opportunities emerge in every individual every time there is a lack of fulfillment in the workplace:

1. TALENT – Knowing Natural Talent
2. SYSTEMS – Thriving in the Environment
3. RESOURCES – Leveraging Key Tools
4. NETWORK – Proactive Collaborating
   SKILLS – Grow Where it Matters

Be it others or yourself, keep in mind blindspots are inevitable. Meaning just because you figured it out in one job or stage of your career does NOT mean you will not see the problem again.

Our side and rearview mirrors are in our vehicles for an ONGOING purpose!

Now, let's get into the details of each blindspot, how it shows up in the real world and what to do about it.

1. TALENT BLINDSPOT.

When people have a Talent Blindspot, they:
- feel insecure.
- are indecisive to act on what matters most to them.
- may project arrogantly.

We all define talent differently. For the sake of a positive work mindset, I'll share my definition.

Talent is what every person (yes, every person) inherently has.

We tend to see talent as a great thing when people are winning or experiencing success, but in the absence of such things, we see it as a weakness, stubbornness or worse, a character flaw.

We may even see it as "no big deal" but recognize them as obvious character traits. Examples:
- She talks a lot.
- They overanalyze.
- She never guesses.
- He always follows the rules.
- She is always changing things just because.

When we're happy in our work, we know what we do well, we're doing it well, and people know what we do well and that's exactly what they're (usually) coming to us for.

Unfortunately, too many of us don't have a full understanding of our FULL talent, or what I've started referring to as the soul, crux, or DNA of talent. Meaning talent is deeper than the skill everyone sees, and it's not limited to any one industry or department.

No matter where you go, there it will be.

Like your shadow with one key difference. Our shadow follows us. Our talent should LEAD us.

A person who is good at accounting may be great at spotting errors deep down. The spotting error's part is the talent, not accounting. I am not making light of accounting, however there are some accountants who HATE the auditing part and would love to farm it out and spend more time being client facing.

See what I mean by the talent not being limited to an industry or a department?

Talent is the desire, the pull of the universe, the OBSESSION you will NEVER EVER BE DONE WITH.

Leverage your talent and you'll be engaged and fulfilled. Waste it, or have it questioned regularly, and you'll feel attacked and out of your element.

(Note - there are many ways to go about fleshing out one's talent).

Personality assessments are very popular and can be useful; unfortunately, they can also be very limiting. Great start but terrible finish when it comes to exploring what people are really naturally good at!

This is not to make light of such tools; they improve communication, sales techniques, relationships, etc. However, vehicles providing perspective on motivation, personal interest, natural bias is crucial and often NOT correlated to behavioral based metrics for too many of us.

When you get a clear insight on what personal biases and priorities exist, it is a game changer.

A few signs of someone seeing their talent fully. They:
- can ARTICULATE it clearly and uniquely.
- actively INVEST (no waiting) in opportunities to express it.
- welcome the talents of OTHERS that complement theirs.

A few concepts that bring clarity to the talent blindspot:

Interpersonal Competence* - Effectively communicating, building rapport and relating well to all kinds of people - not in a faux professional manner, genuinely as equals, human to human.

Internal Acumen* - An understanding of yourself just for being you (many of us struggle here), your roles (the job(s) we accept or resist) and your future (where you are headed). Knowing the differences, as well as the effect one has on the others.

Paraphrased from TTI Success Insights Acumen and 25 DNA Soft Skills.

Even when a person has an idea of what they are good at, they may struggle to articulate, and therefore express, it regularly. Which is crucial for the next blindspot...

2. SYSTEMS BLINDSPOT.

When people have a Systems Blindspot, they:

- feel they are wasting time and energy.
- are burned out.
- allow their downtime to fuel resentment versus progress.

Frustrated people are unaware of how unaware they are of the workplace they're operating in.

It's not ignorance; rather it's mixing up their valid opinions of their jobs from the facts of their job, department, company, industry, region, etc.

I imagine being in court, my career on trial and answering questions with all the FACTS of my job only to constantly be interrupted any time my opinion slips in.

There's a time for that questioning, but they are two different things, and I don't want to piss off the honorable Judge Judy.

Fact v. Opinion.

One is not better than the other but when frustrated, we get them twisted.

Example. To be stuck in rush hour traffic is rarely on someone's to do list, and yet many of us end up surviving long waits due to accidents and other byproducts of large economies.

But to be mad at traffic is silly. We know better. We know at 3 p.m., traffic starts and the longer we wait, it gets worse (until much later when it gets better).

FACTS.

Our opinion, however, still matters, but we can impact that more than we give ourselves credit. The music selection, the temperature of the vehicle (hopefully!) and whatever else. And yet, how often do we take accountability of what we can control in unfortunate, but totally predictable circumstances?

Talent is the "ah-ha" feel-good stuff of coaching. Systems is the blindspot where we spend the most work in personal coaching.

That is why successful athletes have coaches. The athlete does the physical work and shows up, but a good coach helps the athlete see the bigger picture, variables, obstacles and unplanned moments. The only way successful she/they win is by understanding the systemic bigger picture better than their peers in real time.

I want to say "Chess not Checkers" here, but I will not (even though I just did), the analogy is perfect, but I think we may not do it justice. Chess implies thinking a lot of movies ahead, which is great. Where we sell it short is when we just think of the pieces and the tangible game itself.

Poker v. solitaire may be a more suitable comparison.

Poker is not solely about the hand you are dealt. It is reading the entire table, including the human beings who may have to pee or are tired of losing and ready to make a rash decision. It is factoring ALL the things to win the pot.

In modern times, people are spending a lot more time on self-awareness, and likely everyone and their mother have taken some personality assessment. But...

The average person still lacks healthy insights to better understand their regular environment.

Personally, I think that's why therapists may be more popular and acceptable than ever. I'm all for it!

But for those of us not ready for that kind of vulnerability, constructively breaking down and separating our personal opinions from fact about our jobs is key to taking control of what we can.

When frustrated with our work, we forget the laws of the jungle. Or we twist them into things that hold us back more than advance our goal. That is why it is SO imperative to have someone you can trust to solicit feedback.

We are bleeding into the 4th blindspot, Network, a bit. For the sake of the Systems Blindspot, consider how much more effective you are at navigating a journey with others who are more aware than you and you can trust to give constructive insight and feedback.

Now consider being surrounded by others who throw gas on the burning fire that are your workplace delusions.

Now consider being surrounded by others who UNINTENTIONALLY feed your delusions, peers, friends and family who are actively not helping you see the truth.

Consider being alone, or worse, surrounded by no one you can trust. How hard is it to see anything for what it really is?

44

We all are in constant flux with our jobs.

Even if you have the best job ever, it not only can change but will.

It has already.

Go on, go check. I am not going anywhere.

Are you back?

Why did things change at all, and how do I know what change is to come? Can I control the change?

You know the answer! You could. Well, sort of. Not really.

Think of it like GPS on our phones. If you want to get to your destination, you first need an address, right? Nope.

Modern technology has allowed us to be lazy and forget the convenience of big brother always knowing where we are via our phones while we navigate space and time. Of course, you need a destination, but what we forget is that our devices already know where we are first. Our destination's address is actually step two; to get THERE, we first need to know where HERE is.

Not understanding the systems you are in is 100% of your frustrations and fears.

We want to control it versus respect it. He rode the elephant. He did not drive it.

And for you animal lovers out there, if "he" was a jerk and whacked the elephant, he still did not drive the elephant. He forced it and one day that elephant is going to step on him.

Wanting to control things we have no business controlling is the pain.

Fulfillment comes in accepting and finding respect for the thing regardless of what is.

Nature is a great example. Hurricanes. Tornadoes. Tsunamis. Disease.

When we cannot find respect for the things, we will get trampled by it.

Yes, knowing ourselves is very helpful and key, but it's about more than where we are going. Where we are currently is actually more important to improvement. That starts with understanding the system you are in.

It's about a survival technique I once heard an expert give. If you're lost and don't know where you are, take a knee, catch your breath and acknowledge where the sun is. This will tell you how much light and time you have to get to a safe place. (I'm paraphrasing, but you get it!).

Know yourself and you can survive.
But know yourself, and your system, and you will thrive.

Think back to the 3 Reasons We Work chapter. Does the Talent/Systems dynamic takes on new light?

Consider this analogy. A person's talent is like a seed. Put in the right environment - water, sun and soil – and a seed thrives into the plant they're destined to be. If any of those things are lacking, growth could still occur but full potential is unlikely to be reached.

Now we see the awesome power of terrariums!

*Note creative freedom to decorate one's cubicles does not equate to the awesome power of a terrarium.

Growth is not as simple as "work hard". Hard work or grit is not unique to each seed; hard work is likely to come from the seed (talent) which has found the right environment (system) to thrive.

46

Once people figure out how their Talent and Systems blindspots, the next three blindspots start to work themselves out. They're easier to see and prioritize, so less time will be spent on explaining.

A few signs of someone who is seeing their system blindspot fully, they:

- can separate FACT from their OPINION of the system they are in.
- use the system to their ADVANTAGE.
  bridge the current system to where they IDEALLY want to be.

A few concepts that bring clarity to this blindspot:

Time and Priority Management - Knowing what is vital and proactively handling the details within the time you committed. This includes NOT reacting to everything and constantly putting fires out. You get points for that, just not here.

External Acumen - An understanding of people, accepting the how and why others prefer to operate aka their talent, not judging them. You recognize problems, seeing the practical and troubleshooting to get a desired outcome, not excuse making, planning, strategically anticipating long term outcomes. You know the differences, as well as the effect one has on the others.

Telling Time - Not in the literal sense, but the long term. The clearer you see a system, the better timing you can have - beat traffic, ask for a raise, call the client, make the leap on Super Mario World, etc.

In fact, when people are unclear on Talent or the concept of blindspots in general, I'll often see the next blindspots really abused or leveraged to disappointing results.

But once someone has a good idea of their GPS, their Systems Blindspot, the next three blindspots – Resources, Network, and Skills – are usually met with enthusiasm and the elusive GRIT so many of us want to see in others, if not ourselves.

3. RESOURCES BLINDSPOT

When people have a Resources Blindspot, they:
- point fingers at others who waste their own resources.
- make excuses for their lacking outcomes.
- avoid necessary resources they will inevitably have to address.

What are the tools, data and knowledge you have at your fingertips?

Tools are what many people confuse with this book's version of "talent." Tools, being the tangible things, we do and the marketable stuff we know or can do (but don't necessarily love doing). The resume stuff. The 80wpm, six sigma certified, kung fu grip, etc.

What do you need to get from your current place to your destination? That's the blindspot concept we're exploring here. And often, it can be a laundry list of tangible tools, technical software, or some knowledge expertise/certification needed.

Some of us use these tools well and leverage them to their fullest. Others, undervalue or underappreciated them or worse – forget they exist entirely. Sometimes, it's a matter of drawing on the resources that are meant for something else but could help you in your work.

Let's look at the resources of CRMs (Customer Resource Management software). Sales reps either use their

CRM to get big results or they don't and see it as a time suck.

With resources, it's less a matter of using the right tools, and more so a matter of stopping the abuse of the right/wrong ones.

(Shout out to all the machines at the gym we use ineffectively, when our real goal is just to drop 10lbs and look good in our jeans!).

Example. Ask a group of 20-somethings which app in their phone they waste the most time on, and you will get very similar answers (Instagram, Facebook, etc.). These are not necessarily causing anyone harm, but they may definitely create regret or guilt in the amount of time invested.

The app itself isn't the problem; it's what they get (or don't get from it) that's worth recognizing. In fact, it's easy to see how technology can be leveraged once a person has a better idea of their destination relative to their current situation. "Post for the job you want!"

Bluntly put: you are either using the tool or you are the tool.

A few signs someone sees their resources effectively, they:
- rewarded with ROI of the resource.
- make and protect the time necessary to reap the benefits.
- see how a resource can play into their TALENT.

A few concepts that bring clarity to this blindspot:

Personal Accountability - Owning your actions, not blaming your circumstances but using them.

Thinking Practically - An ability to identify and SOLVE problems, not complain and theorize.

Gardening/Gambling - Not in the literal sense, but the long term of making a planting a seed or hedging a bet. The clearer you see how a resource fits into a system, the better the ROI of planting a tree today, doubling down on the odds, using the "fire flower" instead of the "Tanooki Suit" to defeat Bowser.

One more point I want to make, using CRMs as an example. Ambitious sales performers are regularly the ones resisting such tools, taking their own shortcuts because they do not see the ROI.

In other words, they don't see how it can possibly lead them to their destination? Are they right?

A New Work Mindset helps them figure it out.

5. NETWORK BLINDSPOT

When people have a Network Blindspot, they:
- struggle to articulate what they want aka their Talent.
- connect with the WRONG people.
- may connect with the RIGHT people, the WRONG way.

By no means do I consider myself an expert in the actual hustle that is building a network in the traditional sense or the modern technological sense. However, I am very experienced in how human beings tend to undervalue the people they ALREADY know.

Are you connecting with the right people in the right way?

What the hell does that even mean? Well, it means nothing if you have no idea of the destination you want to arrive at. See the pattern here?

As it relates to the Network Blindspot, what I've seen often are others not articulating to the RIGHT people/audience/clients about how they can actually help them.

While it is about talking to the right people - see SYSTEMS blindspot - it is also about doing it in a way that you (the GPS-er) feel most comfortable and accountable.

Example. Any time a self-described introvert or shy person asks how they should meet new people or market themselves; I tell them to volunteer for whatever event seems interesting. This takes all the risk out of it because you're there early, you're given instructions and by default, you'll meet people and give immediate value.

Go from there, or go home. By then you've already tested the waters, and you can make a decision you're comfortable with.

So, here's where the Talent and System blindspots really matter. If someone does not know what they are good at, nor do they know where they want to be going, why the hell would they want to go out and talk to anyone?

Because it is their job, duh.

But when you know what you are good at, excited to share it, or more importantly, excited to share about the problems you solve for others, what's more fun than interacting with people who want said problems solved?

Nothing!

Really, it's a grand ol' time.

Okay, I'm being a little silly because at first it can be awkward, and it feels totally odd for many. Like Bambi taking his first steps. But give me any person who is clear on what they do well and who they can do it for, and I will show you someone ready for a quality conversation.

The flipside are those people who just hit up anyone and everyone. They are often enabling great fun conversations that go nowhere with well-meaning people, who had no idea what they meant and how it mattered to them. (Guilty!)

Good networking is about more than just knowing who you are and where you're going. It's about empathy.

Do you understand how YOU feel, excited or not? Are you tuned in to you? Do you understand how these potential contacts currently feel before you have reached out? While you are reaching out? Do you know how they feel after you have reached out?

Or have you understood why they will never again reach out or possibly be excited to connect back with you again?

Empathy is more popular than ever, but still underserved because it is HARD. It requires effort in admitting "I don't know, I'll ask." Stop and consider that you may not have the answer about another person's life. And your assumption as it relates to your life does not apply at the moment.

Gasp!

Empathy when done EFFECTIVELY (not faux politely), looks a lot like a great admirable sales experience. Not the kind of sleazy situation we can all imagine or have experienced.

It's about understanding WHO you actually can help, letting them know it, and then reverse connecting with others who can help you on their terms along the way.

A few signs that someone sees their network effectively are they:

- confidently and clearly ARTICULATE their wants to the right people.
- receive NEW opportunities, via referrals, often. actively seek out qualified HELP.

A few concepts that bring clarity to this blindspot:

Emotional Intelligence - minding emotions to be EFFECTIVE, by being aware of your own emotions and their effect on desired outcomes and being aware of the emotions of others and adjusting to arrive at a desired outcome.

Sales/Persuasion - The good kind to be clear, not the hustle mind-jacking that comes to mind for some. "Good" sales or persuasion is the art of affecting someone's decision, opinions or thinking. It is the difference between a lecturer and a teacher who guides a student to an informed decision maker.

Good networking takes both an understanding of yourself and the other side's point of view. Once you are clear on that, this next and final blindspot almost reveals itself.

5. SKILLS.

When people have a Skills Blindspot, they:
- overestimate what they NEED work on.
- undervalue what they ENJOY working on.
- are "busy" but not progressing to their true desired outcomes.

The best of the best are never done. The most fulfilled are never done growing.

The arrogant think they have it all figured out or triple down on RESOURCES to grow rather than skills to improve.

"Everyone is stupid except me." - Homer Simpson

Unlike Talent and Resources, Skills blindspots are about improving in areas that intentionally drive the work that matters to the work you care about! It is different from learning a resource (okay okay, I should've called this the Soft/Personal Skills Blindspot, but I liked the one-word titles)!

To grow your skills is to work on those things that are hard to measure but truly matter to getting the next milestone.

Planning and organizing, leadership and persuasion are all examples of next-level skills.

People misuse their energies in not just avoiding skill development but also over-developing.

A popular example: college students. There is such a thing as too much studying. Did you really need the A+, when you have a solid A and still need to land that internship, experience more and learn outside the classroom? Maybe an argument could be made for the A+, but why? If it is necessary, it drives something bigger than the grade; what is being avoided that helps the bigger mission?

Just because we work hard does not mean it is smart or effective. And differently put, just because it appears "smart" does not mean it is effective in the grander goal.

Again, when you understand how your Talent relates to the System, the resources, network and skills start to naturally appear.

My advice for most people is simplify this blindspot into 2 SOFT skills to improve:

Talent Fit - Something you enjoy doing, you're already pretty great at it. If it was a class, you'd have a 95%, aim for an A++.

Inevitable Procrastinating - Something you hate doing but you know will help you advance. If it was a class, you'd have an F. Just show up, aim for a D-, aim to improve 1%, no more than 5%.

Example. I love interviewing. But priority management? I need it and must force it.

I love talking and making observations. It's the 1s and 0s of my own TALENT. So, like 90% of the world, I started a podcast. I see it like this: my podcast is a SYSTEM I believe caters to my talent naturally. I love interviewing and coming up with nuanced episodes and even when I am drained, I get revved up within a few minutes doing the above.

Even my worst episodes are fond memories, and in my best ones, I see ways to improve immediately and want more. So, I do more. Whereas, the technical aspect I dread and will not do unless I have real deadlines/priorities that matter.

Going back and listening to the same episode to edit, clip and post on social is NOT fun for me in the least, but if I want to share the fruits of my labor of love, I must do the thing. So, I move that needle just a bit, and in a few months' time, I have improved at both immensely. BOTH move the needle immediately to becoming a content creator, host, etc.

The idea is #1 is easy and will get you going, and #2 may still be a drag. If it is mentally viewed as "easier" (i.e., doing 1 push up a day), you do it. As long as you see how it serves your talent.

A few signs someone sees their skills effectively, they:

- intentionally take risks with immediate consequences/rewards.
- learn from failures and get NEW desired results.
- have/closer to their MOST desired opportunities.

A lone concept that brings clarity to this blindspot:

Goal Orientation - Achieving an outcome, regardless of circumstances. That is, it: your goal is achieved, or it is not. The skill, soft skill, competency is NOT the goal, it is a means to accomplishing the goal.

I believe everyone wants to work harder and spend more time/money – on work that matters to them. That last part is the tricky part. Many people lose sight of, or never grasp, what is most important to them.

When you are clear, skills not only improve, you are closer to your desired outcome aka being able to be in your talent. You feel accountable, in control, focused, and maybe even a little nervous but the good kind. Kind of like a fist bump (more on that later).

Fulfillment is a unique personal journey and spans well beyond these 5 blindspots. However, these universally have applied to everyone who's "happy", "loves their work", finds "flow states", etc.

Here's a summary of what it looks like when things are in rhythm, with...

TALENT you,

- KNOWS/BELIEVE your Talent.
- Can ARTICULATE it.
- INVEST in it.

SYSTEMS you,
- Know where you CURRENTLY are.
- Know where your talent will THRIVE.
- BRIDGE the gap.

RESOURCES you,
- KNOW the effective tools.
- PRIORITIZE the tools.
- LEVERAGE the tools.

NETWORK you,
- WHY you want to connect with others.
- Know WHO wants to connect.
- Connect EFFECTIVELY.

SKILLS you,
- Know your MENTAL GAP to your goals.
- PRIORITIZE development.
- You SELF MOTIVATE.

Find a disgruntled person and I guarantee 1, if not all five blindspots apply.

Such is life. For those of us lucky to have found fulfillment, it's not guaranteed to last. Life happens, industry shifts, markets rise and fall, pandemics, wars, new bosses, mergers - cue Billy Joel's "We Didn't Start the Fire".

Even if you have the perfect dream job... full engagement that thrills because constantly calls for your best talent (only) aligned with your heart's deepest wants, is just unlikely.

Change is constant and will disrupt even the best of times.

Course correcting is simply being first aware change happens, but then resilient to do something about the disruption.

Resilience, at least in the workplace, is about understanding our inevitable blindspots and being conscious of how our reasons to work will fluctuate based on – but not limited to – our leaders, our work, and ourselves.

Be aware, be resilient.
Be resilient, give more fist bumps.

Chapter 5
Simply Put, Get More Fist Bumps

Let us dissect and deconstruct one more thing – the fist bump.

Having a great work mindset means having days when work is riveting and crazy and, if you could, you would give the job a real fist bump. Maybe several. If it has been a while, bear with me, recall a time where a situation called for a celebration and you, at the very least, felt the DESIRE to celebrate it with someone else.

I am referring to REAL fist bumps, not lame, annoying one's to make someone go away!

The fist bump when you "pulled it off", you and someone else took a risk and by golly it worked!

(If you are not a fan of fist bumps or human contact swap in something else where you FEEL it in your bones, your heart-mind, the FEELING is what matters most!)

Would you like to know how you get more REAL fist bumps?

Would you like to know how to get others to WANT to GIVE more real bumps at work?

Of course, you do. Otherwise, you probably quit reading a long time ago.

Then you must deconstruct YOUR fist bump, using two similar but different concepts:

- DISC
- Motivators

This is an abbreviated version, and for the sake of work mindsets, I am taking liberties. If you'd like more information, workshops, training – reach out.

For now, look at the DISC chart" HOW people prefer to communicate*.

*You can apply other popular assessing tools here. However, most assessments, while they may claim personality or other deep measurements, relate mainly to behavioral preference, NOT anything else. I am open to being corrected, but that is not the focus at the moment.]

C	D
compliance – perfection, accurate, analytical	dominance – direct, daring, forceful
"I prefer to do things right the first time, no mistakes."	*"I prefer to go fast, go big, and get results!"*

S	I
steadiness – patient, passive, listener	influence – enthusiastic, trusting, charming
"I prefer to be careful and mindful of others ."	*"I prefer to make new friends and share ideas!"*

Pick two for yourself that represents you at your best!

If you are unsure, that is okay. Reflect back on times when you were doing your most exciting work, or perhaps when your work felt the EASIEST.

Now, look at the MOTIVATORS chart - WHY people ENGAGE or resist**

**A true clear insight to what motivates you rather than just what you're good at or how you like to do things is CRUCIAL to getting to the fist bump moment, either for you or others. I will go as far to say that it is MORE foundational that DISC or any other tool. Unlike other tools, we can adapt and learn new skills. Motivators, as used here, is more about

personal conviction. You cannot compromise that. It is the REASON we get upset.

"Nobody puts Juanie in a corner!" - My inner monologue.

THEORY	TRADITIONS
Driven to seek information and facts.	Driven to protect a defined system for living.
"I want to discover new truths."	*"I want to protect my beliefs."*
OTHERS	SELF
Driven to help others.	Driven to control one's destiny and/or lead others.
"I want to help other people."	*"I want to lead myself/others."*
EXPRESSIVE	ECONOMICS
Driven to maximize time and resources.	Driven to maximize time and resources.
"I want to design pleasant experiences."	*"I want to capitalize on opportunity."*

Pick 3 for yourself that resonate/represent you when you're doing your best!

If you are unsure, that is okay!
Reflect on what PISSES you off or STRESSES you out. Negative indicators can be more revealing than positive indicators. Imagine if you could NOT have the motivator or something oppressed it, which would make you rage!?
Good. [You can stop raging.]

Now, hold out your hand like you are five-years-old telling me, "I am this many years old."

Happy New Work Mindset birthday! Repeat after me, *"I am doing my best work when I am…"*

1. [Insert 1st DISC choice], wiggle your thumb.
2. [Insert 2nd DISC choice] wiggle your pointer.
3. [Insert 1st Motivator choice] wiggle your middle.
4. [Insert 2nd DISC choice], wiggle your ring finger.
5. [Insert 3rd DISC choice], wiggle your pinky.

Now make a fist. Repeat what you just said… Do you feel like bumpin' fists, homie?

If I gave you a job and asked you to be "you", to be 5 of 5, would doing that work YOU way interest you?

The work could be with any department or even an industry you despise. But if YOU gotta be YOU, in all you do, that work would FEEL different.

Sounds good, right?

That is exactly what is happening for other people, at least when they legit feel great about their work and truly want to bump fist or do whatever their soul is screaming to do.

Realistically though, is that most workplaces?

I think it can be, but likely is not.

Not everyone's job, person or situation naturally wants us to be 100% us all the time.

See the 3 Reasons We Work chapter:

1. <2 fingers you are SURVIVING, "I have to"
2. 3-4 you are SAVING, "I can…"
    5 you are SERVING, "I choose to…"

Knowing what makes you want to fist bump does not guarantee all the fist bump feels. [Definitely a good start!].

Hold your hand back out again, this time think of your job and ask yourself how many fingers (behaviors/motivators) your CURRENT WORK REGULARLY asks and needs of you?

What about your peers?

Consider the nuance of each high performer's fist?

Low performers?

Low performers probably aren't fist bumping too often. In fact, if they're surviving or worse having a really bad day, only one finger might be greeting others...

Take a guess which one....

Our work mindsets are simply about how we see our work and relate to doing the work.

While humans are vastly different, we have our REASONS and BLINDSPOT at work.

Daily fist bumps are the bi-product of a good culture where the LEADER's relationship with their work is a blueprint for everyone else.

Fake fist bumps cultivate the cultures of entitlement, burn out and toxicity.

Toxic positivity is not my word but it is real and I hope you are not an offender.

If you want a better work culture, start with your own mindset.

If you are responsible for the culture, start with your own mindset and seek the fist. (Also, an excellent tagline to a Summer Action flick!)

REAL DEAL fist bumps.

***

To come back full circle, let us revisit the first question, "Why Can't They Do Their Damn Jobs?"
Because, they are...

Lazy.
Stupid.
Young.
Entitled.
Old.
Ignorant.
Conservative.
Liberal.
(Fill in your go to judgement here.)
(Insert other's judgments about you here.)

When those shortsighted answers are given, we are NOT leading, we are judging.
I lean into my own hypocrisy as I shout... THAT. IS. STUPID!

For leaders, fulfillment seekers, judging others is an absolute waste of time. Judging others feels good in the moment, sarcasm and snark taste good going down, but those empty calories haunt us.

Those empty calories are haunting those who are meeting you with their middle fingers raised right back at you.

That is on them. The question is: what are you going to do the next time you are...

Taking responsibility for your CULTURE, what you can and cannot impact regarding the workplace. Be honest in how you or other leaders relate to THEIR roles and set the tone for others?

Understanding your team's REASONS they work in developing them to step up and adapt to their jobs and the future of business?

Hiring for that mission critical executive or entry level high performer and their BLINDSPOTS?

A New Work Mindset is about REFRESHING how we and others approach our leaders, our jobs, and ourselves at work, and the inevitability of things not going to plan.

How many fist bumps or single fingers will meet you daily is up to you.

"Attitude is everything." is a wonderful quote but means jackshit when someone is miserable. Avoid being like a doctor who says to his sick patients, "Well just be healthy. Thanks, please remember to pay your copay on the way out."

Read this book, listen to the podcast, tell me I am wrong.

Whatever you do, do better at work.